Library of Congress Cataloging-in-Publication Data

Thomson, Ruth.
All About Colors.

(My first easy and fun books)
Bibliography: p.
Summary: Picnicking bears enjoy the green field, yellow bananas, pink cake, and other colorful aspects of their
outing.
[1. Bears--Fiction. 2. Color--Fiction. 3. Picnicking--Fiction] I. Ward, Deborah, ill. II. Title. III. Series: Thomson, Ruth.
My first easy and fun books.
PZ7.T38Co   1987   [E]   87-42588
ISBN 1-55532-337-5
ISBN 1-55532-312-X (lib. bdg.)

North American edition first published in 1987 by
Gareth Stevens, Inc.
7221 West Green Tree Road Milwaukee, WI 53223, USA

Original text copyright © 1986 by Ruth Thomson.
Supplementary text copyright © 1987 by Gareth Stevens, Inc.
Illustrations copyright © 1986 by Deborah Ward.

First published as *Colours* in the United Kingdom by Walker Books Ltd.

Typeset by Web Tech, Inc., Milwaukee. Printed in Italy.
Series Editor: MaryLee Knowlton.

1 2 3 4 5 6 7 8 9 92 91 90 89 88 87

MY FIRST EASY AND FUN BOOKS

ALL ABOUT

colors

By Ruth Thomson
Illustrated by Deborah Ward

Gareth Stevens Publishing
Milwaukee

brown

James, George, and Patti
are three **brown** bears.

They are going on a picnic.
"Let's go, slow pokes," says Patti.

green

The bears find a pretty **green**
meadow. Patti opens the gate.

blue

"This is a good spot," says James,
helping George spread the **blue** cloth.

"Not on me!" says poor Patti.

white

"A **white** plate for
you and you," says Patti.

"And a polka dot plate for me."

yellow

"Yummy! **Yellow** bananas,"
James says. "And pears, too."

"Pass the honey, please,"
Patti says to George.

red

James takes a big **red** apple.
He rubs it to make it shiny.

"What do you think of my
red earrings?" asks Patti.

orange

"**Orange** juice, anyone?"
George says.

"Look!" cries Patti.
"Here comes David Bear!"

pink

"Strawberry peppermint cake!"
sighs James. "I think I'll eat it all!"

"I think <u>I'll</u> eat it all!" says David Bear.
He jumps up and grabs the **pink** cake.

black

Off go the bears!
Patti falls into the **black**berry bushes.

"Come back! I'll share!" James cries.

purple

Patti is up again,
waving the **purple** umbrella.

James tickles David. The cake flies
in the air. George makes the save!

Find the colors.

"Exercise before dessert
makes me hungry!" says David Bear.

"Have some cake," laugh the other bears. "Don't mind if I do," says David.

brown	
green	
blue	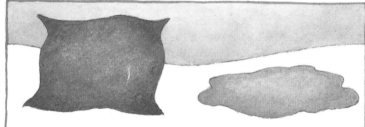
white	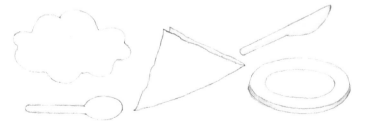
yellow	

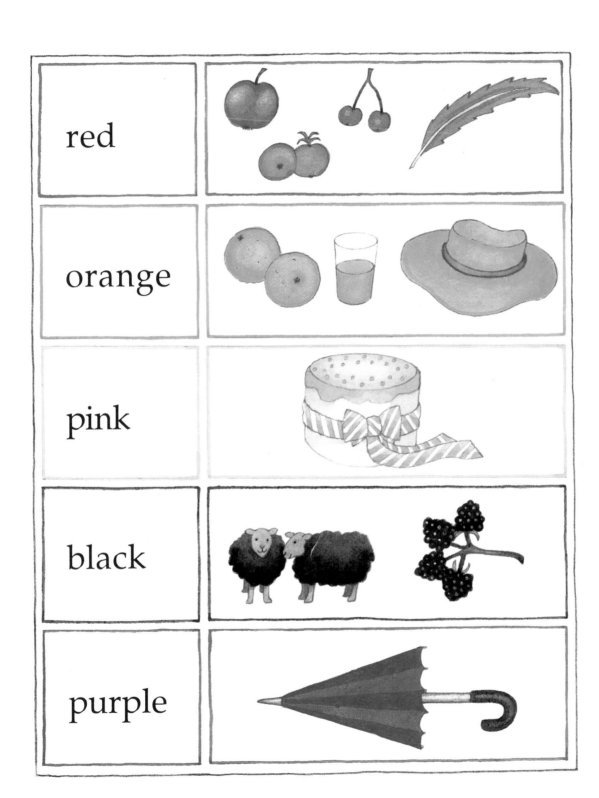

red

orange

pink

black

purple

Things To Do

1. Name the colors of foods in your refrigerator.

2. Write red, blue, yellow, purple, and green at the top of columns on a piece of paper. Look at a large colorful picture in a magazine or book for one minute. Turn the picture over. Write as many things as you can remember under each color column.

3. Look through magazines or catalogs for pictures that are in color. Cut them out and paste them on paper to make a color book of your own.

4. Count the number of red cars that pass your house in five minutes. Then count black or blue or gray. What color cars do you see most often?

5. Take a walk around your house with a piece of paper and a pencil. On the piece of paper, make four columns. At the top of each, write a color. Look for things of that color and write them in the proper column. You can do this with friends, too, and see who gets the longest lists.

6. When you start on a car trip, decide what color things to count. Everybody can look for things and call out what they see.

More Books About Colors

Colors. Pienkowski (Little Simon)

Colors. Reiss (Aladdin)

Do You Know Colors? Howard (Random House)

Get Ready: Colors and Shapes. Muntean (Random House/Children's Television Workshop)

Goofy's Book of Colors (Disney/Random House)

Magic of Color. Simon (Lothrop, Lee & Shepard)

Merry-Mouse Counting and Colors Book. Hillman (Doubleday)